methuen | drama

LONDON • NEW YORK • OXFORD • NEW DELHI • SYDNEY

METHUEN DRAMA
Bloomsbury Publishing Plc
50 Bedford Square, London, WC1B 3DP, UK
1385 Broadway, New York, NY 10018, USA

BLOOMSBURY, METHUEN DRAMA and the Methuen Drama logo are trademarks of Bloomsbury Publishing Plc

First published in Great Britain 2019

Cover design: Terry Woodley

Cover image © David Wilson Photography

A catalogue record for this book is available from the British Library.

ISBN: PB: 978-1-3501-0904-9
ePDF: 978-1-3501-0905-6
eBook: 978-1-3501-0906-3

Series: Modern Plays

Typeset by Mark Heslington Ltd, Scarborough, North Yorkshire
Printed and bound in Great Britain

To find out more about our authors and books visit www.bloomsbury.com and sign up for our newsletters.

BLUE

CAST

Jordan Bernarde	Thomas
Sophie Melville	Elin
Gwydion Rhys	Huw
Nia Roberts	Lisa

CREATIVE

Created by	Rebecca Jade Hammond
Written by	Rhys Warrington
Director	Chelsey Gillard
Designer	Oliver Harman
Lighting Designer	Ceri James
Sound Designer	Tic Ashfield
Dramaturg	Matthew Bulgo

PRODUCTION

Producer	Rebecca Jade Hammond
Co-Producer	Chapter
Stage Manager	Bethan Dawson
Production Assistant	Sophie Hughes
BSL Interpreter	Sami Thorpe

MARKETING

Marketing & PR	Chloe Nelkin Consulting & PR
Trailer by	Now in a Minute Productions
Publicity Photograph by	David Wilson Photography
Publicity Design by	Lucas Pardue

SUPPORT IN KIND

Chapter, Dementia UK, Older People's Commissioner for Wales, Ty Hapus, David Wilson Photography, Philip Carne, Christine Carne.

This piece is a co-production between Chippy Lane Productions Ltd and Chapter, kindly supported by Arts Council Wales Cyngor Celfyddau Cymru.

Rhys Warrington | Writer

Rhys trained as an actor at the Royal Conservatoire of Scotland and *BLUE* is his debut play as a professional writer.

Acting work includes: *The Mousetrap* (West End/Mumbai); *Great Expectations* (West End); *Praxis Makes Perfect* (National Theatre Wales); *How the Other Half Loves* (Torch Theatre); *WiLd!* (Tutti Frutti/iPAY USA); *Love Steals Us From Loneliness* (Chippy Lane Productions/Camden People's Theatre/Chapter).

Chelsey Gillard | Director

Chelsey is a freelance director and Co-Artistic Director of PowderHouse (*Company in Residence at Sherman Theatre*) and recent script reading panelist for the Theatre Uncut Political Playwriting Award.

Chelsey was previously Associate Director at The Other Room and has received the Young Directors Development Award from Pontardawe Arts Centre and the JMK Regional Assistant Director Bursary.

Directing work includes: *[BLANK]* (Sherman Youth Theatre); *The Burton Taylor Affair* (Oran Mor, Glasgow); *My Name is Rachel Corrie* (Graphic and The Other Room) and *Constellation Street* (The Other Room, co-directed with Dan Jones) which won Best Production at the Wales Theatre Awards 2017.

Rebecca Hammond | Creator & Producer

Rebecca is an actress, writer, producer and graduate of Royal Central School of Speech & Drama, Bath Spa University and Artistic Director of Chippy Lane Productions Ltd.

Acting work includes: *Silent Witness* (BBC); *Doctors* (BBC); *Trollied* (Sky 1); *Happiness Ltd* (Theatre Royal Plymouth, Salisbury Playhouse); *Love Steals Us From Loneliness* (Chippy Lane Productions/Camden People's Theatre/Chapter); *Heresies* (Bristol Old Vic); *A Streetcar Named Desire* (The Egg Theatre Bath); *Triforce Monologue Slam Finalist* (Cardiff/London).

Writing work includes: *MidnightMiracle* (Amazon Prime); Pontardawe ScriptSlam Finalist 2017 and longlisted for Papatango and Theatre503 Writing Award 2018.

Producing work includes: BLUE; Love Steals Us From Loneliness; Chippy & Scratch Shorts Night 2016–2018; Chippy Lane's Rehearsed Readings and Chippy Lane's Podcast (Chippy Lane Productions/ Itunes).

Jordan Bernarde | Thomas

Jordan trained at Royal Welsh College of Music & Drama.

Theatre includes: *Crazy Gary's Mobile Disco* (Waking Exploits); Nominated Best Actor Wales Theatre Awards, *As Is* (Finborough Theatre); Nominated Best Male "Offie's", *Little Dogs* (Frantic Assembly/NTW); *The Passion* (NTW); 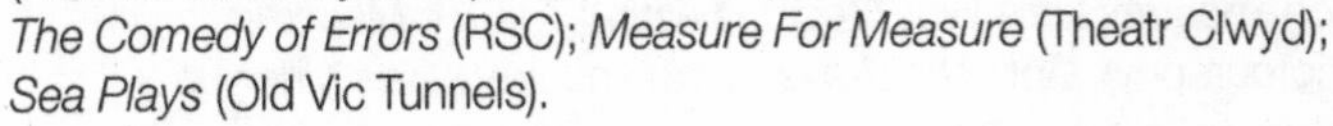
The Comedy of Errors (RSC); *Measure For Measure* (Theatr Clwyd); *Sea Plays* (Old Vic Tunnels).

Television & film includes: *Rabbi Knows Better* (Cando); *The Stand* (Corrwg Productions); *The Gospel of Us* (Rondo); *Da Vinci's Demons* (Starz); *The Hanged Man* (BBC Worldwide); *First Light* (BBC/Lion TV).

Radio includes: *Chippy Lane's Podcast* (Chippy Lane Productions); *The Blast of War*, *Pink Mist*, *Past Masters* (BBC Radio 4).

Sophie Melville | Elin

Sophie trained as an actress at Royal Welsh College of Music & Drama.

Sophie is the winner of The Stage Award for Acting Excellence (2015), Winner of My Theatre Mates Best Solo Performance (2017) and twice winner of Wales Theatre Awards and nominated for an Evening Standard Award (2016) and Drama Desk Award in (2018).

Theatre includes: *Iphigenia In Splott* (Sherman Theatre/National Theatre/Schaubuhne/59E59 New York); *'Tis Pity She's a Whore, See How They Run, The Shape of Things* (Theatre by the Lake); *Romeo and Juliet* (Sherman Theatre); *Insignificance, Under Milk Wood* (Theatr

Clwyd); *Blackbird* (The Other Room Theatre); 2066 (Almeida Theatre); Low Level Panic (The Orange Tree); *The Divide, Pagans* (Old Vic); *No One Will Tell Me How to Start a Revolution* (Hampstead Theatre); *Pops* (Young Vic); *Close Quarters* (Sheffield Crucible).

Television includes: *The Missing 2*; *Telling Tales*; *The Left Behind* (BBC).

Gwydion Rhys | Huw

Theatre includes: *The Village Social* (National Theatre Wales); *Pornography, Crazy Gary's Mobile Disco* (Waking Exploits); *The Tempest, Tir Sir Gar* (Theatr Genedlaethol Cymru); *Windongs of the Blessed Bay* (Theatr Cadair); *Swansea's Three Night Blitz* (Swansea Grand); *Iphigenia in Orem, Wolf Tattoo* (Company of Sirens); *The Wood, One Man Two Guvnors* (Torch Theatre); *Little Wolf* (Lucid Theatre); *To Kill a Machine* (Scriptography); *Only The Brave* (Soho Theatre/Wales Millenium Centre).

Television & film includes: *Tir* (Joio); *Cara Fi* (Touchpaper); *Parch, 35 Diwrnod* (Boom); *Hinterland, Hidden* (BBC/S4C); *Macaroni, Albie a Noa* (S4C); *Daniels* (ARC Films); *The Rebels* (Tornado Studios).

Nia Roberts | Lisa

Nia is a winner of the BAFTA Cymru Award for Best Actress.

Theatre includes: *Rhith Gan, Esther* (Theatr Genedlaethol Cymru); *Love Steals Us From Loneliness* (National Theatre Wales); *Cynnau Tân, The Get Together* (Sherman Theatre); *Lovely Evening* (Young Vic); *Stone City Blue* (Theatr Clwyd); *Cymbeline, Under Milk Wood* (Wales Theatre Company).

Television & film includes: *The Crown* (Netflix); *Pili Pala* (S4C); *To Provide all People* (BBC); *Craith/Hidden* (S4C/BBC Wales); *Bang* (Joio/S4C/BBC Wales); *Keeping Faith* (S4C/BBC); *Rillington Place, The White Princess, Doctors* (BBC); *35 Diwrnod* (S4C); *Hinterland* (S4C/BBC); *Gifted* (Baby Cow); *Pianissimo* (S4C); *Doctor Who* (BBC);

Collision (Greenlit); *Crash* (Red Planet); *Pen Talar* (Fiction Factory); *Midsomer Murders* (ITV); *Hotel Babylon* (BBC); *Y Pris* (S4C); *Holby City* (BBC); *Border Cafe* (Hartswood Films); *Casualty*, *Score* (BBC); *Lois* (Eryri Films); *Last Summer* (Flicker Book Film/Casm); *Just Jim* (Vox Pictures); *Under Milk Wood* (Fatti Films); *Third Star* (Western Edge Films); *The Facility* (Vertigo Films); *Bridgend* (Blenkov and Schonnermann Pictures); *Patagonia* (Malacara); *Snow Cake* (Revolution Films); *Solomon and Gaenor* (Film Four, Oscar Nominated for Best Foreign Film).

Oliver Harman | Designer

Oliver Harman studied at the Royal Welsh College of Music and Drama (2015) and achieved a BA (Hons) in Theatre Design.

Oliver has worked as Set and Costume Designer for a variety of productions including *FESTIVAL!* (Pentabus Theatre); *A Christmas Carol* (Simply Theatre Productions); *My Name is Rachel Corrie* (Graphic/The Other Room); *Not About Heroes* (Seabright Productions); *The Orator* (Theatre West) and realised the design for *Bordello*, a show part of the Italian 'SALAMARZANA: Festa Medievale'.

He has also production designed the music video for 4th Project and their song *Taking Me Over* (Pixllion). As well as designing, Oliver has worked as Design Assistant on shows such as *The Convert* (The Gate Theatre); *Sleeping Beauty* (The Torch Theatre Company); *Yuri* (Chapter) and *Rosie's War* (Theatr na nÓg). He has also been the design assistant for the previous seasons of 'Outliers' and 'Insomnia' at The Other Room, Cardiff.

Ceri James | Lighting Designer

Theatre includes: *Fel Anifael* (Sherman Theatre); *Tide Whisperer, Roald Dahl City of the Unexpected* and *Lifted by Beauty* (National Theatre Wales); *Mags* (Cwmni Pluen); *Woman of Flowers Video* (Theatr Pena); *Nyrsys, Y Tad, Merch yr Eog and Rhith gân* (Theatr Genedlaethol Cymru); *Anweledig, Mwgsi* (Frân Wen); *BOHO* (Clwyd Theatre Cymru/Hijinx); *The Trials of Oscar Wilde* (Mappa Mundi Theatre); *A Christmas Carol* (Fondazione Haydn di Bolzano e Trento, Italy); *Simplicius Simplicissimus* (Independent Opera, Sadler's Wells); *Belonging* (*Re-Live*); *A Christmas Carol* (Welsh National Opera); *Beneath the Streets*

(Punch Drunk/Hijinx Theatre); *One Man Two Guvnors, One Flew Over the Cuckoo's Nest* (Torch Theatre Company).

Tic Ashfield | Composer & Sound Designer

Tic Ashfield MMus BMus (Hons) (RWCMD) is a BAFTA Cymru Award Winning Composer and Sound Designer based in South Wales.

Tic has created music and sound for numerous projects including work for film, TV, theatre, dance, animation, installation and educational outreach projects. Commissioners and collaborators include BBC 1 Wales, BBC 2, BBC 4, S4C, All3Media, Fiction Factory, Severn Screen, National Theatre Wales, The Other Room Theatre, Omidaze Productions, Winding Snake Productions, Welsh National Opera, Lighthouse Theatre, Joio and Gwyn Emberton Dance. She is a creative team member at both John Hardy Music and Winding Snake Productions. Tic has led music workshops for companies such as Welsh National Opera and Winding Snake Productions, working with young people from junior school age up to sixth formers. She is also a lecturer in Composition with Technology at RWCMD.

As a composer and sound designer she focuses on using a combination of found sound manipulation and sampling, synthesis and instrumental writing to create bespoke soundworlds, often within collaborative settings.

Matthew Bulgo | Dramaturg

Matthew trained at LAMDA and works as an actor, playwright and dramaturg.

Writing work includes: *Last Christmas* (Dirty Protest/Theatr Clwyd) which subsequently transferred to the Edinburgh Fringe, Soho Theatre and Traverse; *Constellation Street* (The Other Room); *#YOLO* (National Theatre, NT Connections); *The Awkward Years* (The Other Room/Chapter); *The Knowledge* (Royal Court, 'Surprise Theatre' Season); *My Father's Hands* (Paines Plough, Come To Where I'm From).

As an actor, he has worked for Theatr Clwyd, Sherman Theatre, National Theatre Wales, Traverse, Royal & Derngate, Wales Millennium Centre and The Other Room among many others.

Matthew was the recipient of the Best Playwright accolade at the Wales Theatre Awards in both 2015 and 2017.

Bethan Dawson | Stage Manager

Bethan graduated from the Royal Welsh College of Music and Drama in Stage Management in 2011.

Recent theatre credits include: *Close Quarters* (Out of Joint and Sheffield Theatres); *Peggy's Song* and *Come Back Tomorrow* (National Theatre Wales); *The Rise and Fall of Little Voice* (Theatr Clwyd); *Cathy* (Cardboard Citizens); *A Number* and *Seanmhair* (The Other Room); *The Alternativity* (Flossy & Boo); *The Tempest* (Taking Flight Theatre Company); *Looking Through Glass* and *Alix In Wundergarten* (difficult|stage); *Saturday Night Forever* (Aberystwyth Arts Centre).

Bethan also works with Mess Up The Mess, who make brave and awkward theatre by, for and with young people.

Chippy Lane Productions Ltd. (CLP) was founded in 2016 by Rebecca Jade Hammond, a Cardiff-born actor, writer and producer. CLP's primary mission is to promote Welsh and Wales-based theatre and talent, to audiences in and beyond Wales. *'Regional work is important, audiences want to hear stories from everywhere'* (CLP in Arts Scene In Wales, 2016).

CLP is a London-based Welsh company created in response to our research that showed a lack of Welsh work being produced beyond Wales. The arts, in Wales and from Welsh origin, are undergoing change and there is a wealth of excitement for writing, acting and theatre that is new, diverse and vibrant. We achieve our goal by building relationships with established Welsh and Wales-based playwrights, encouraging and producing new work, and reaching out to Welsh communities living inside and outside of Wales. '*The grass roots of Welsh performance are irrepressible*' (CLP in Theatre In Wales, 2018).

At the helm of this company is Artistic Director Rebecca Jade Hammond. Her commitment and dedication to the championing of the Welsh and Wales-based voices has been met with open arms from fellow creatives. Her position and perspective as a Welsh company operating outside of Wales developing work across both Wales and England, bridging the gap between two countries has led to interest from arts media (What's On Stage, GetTheChanceWales, Arts Scene in Wales, Western Mail). Rebecca was also recently recognised as a '100 Women of Wales' 2018 by Wales Arts Review, which highlights women who are ones to watch, and inspiring the arts in Wales.

THE COMPANY

Artistic Director	Rebecca Jade Hammond
Associate Playwright	Jacob Hodgkinson
Production Assistant	Sophie Hughes
Creative Associate	Andrew David
Creative Associate	Sophie Melville
Creative Associate	Rhys Warrington
Company Director	Lucas Pardue

CHAPTER

Chapter Arts Centre

Chapter is a multi-artform arts centre that produces, presents and promotes international art, live performance and film alongside a dynamic social space and a network of more than 30 artists' studios. For nearly fifty years the centre has been the heartbeat of creativity in Cardiff, and continues to support independent creatives on a local and global platform.

With a year-round programme of visual art, film, music, dance, theatre, learning and events and a vibrant café bar serving up delicious food and drink, Chapter has something to offer visitors of all ages and welcomes more than 800,000 visitors each year.

Chapter, Market Road, Canton, Cardiff, Wales, CF5 1QE
t: 029 2030 4400 e: enquiry@chapter.org, www.chapter.org

Company Registration Number: 01005570 | Registered Charity Number: 50081

PRODUCTION ACKNOWLEDGEMENTS

Arts Council Wales, Ben Atterbury, Andrew Bate, Brad Birch, Biscuit Pardue-Hammond, Blackwood Miners' Institute, Matthew Bulgo, Alice Burrows, Philip Carne, Christine Carne, Chapter, Simon Coates, David Wilson Photography, Simon Alun Davies, Dementia Wales, Maggie Dunning, Chelsey Gillard, Hammerpuzzle Theatre Company, Jacob Hodgkinson, Sophie Hughes, Rhys Isaac Jones, Simon Lee, London Welsh Centre, Sophie Melville, National Theatre Wales, Guy O'Donnell, Dom O'Hanlon, Older People Wales, Lucas Pardue, Ri Richards, Marcelo Dos Santos, Ceriann Williams, Sion Daniel Young, Lisa Zahra.

BLUE was first performed on Tuesday 5th February 2019 at Chapter, Cardiff.

The text went to print during rehearsals and may differ from the text in production.

For Kitty Stamp (Nan) the first great storyteller I ever encountered.

– Rebecca Jade Hammond

For Nicola Warrington (Mum), the strongest person I know & John Warrington (Dad), the nickname master.

– Rhys Warrington

BLUE

'How easy it was to lie to strangers, to create with strangers the versions of our lives we imagined.'
Chimamanda Ngozi Adichie

'Little islands are all large prisons; one cannot look at the sea without wishing for the wings of a swallow.'
Richard Francis Burton

Characters

Lisa Williams *(the mother mid 50s)*
Elin Williams *(her daughter mid 20s)*
Huw Williams *(her son early 20s)*
Thomas Stevenson *(a school teacher early 30s, not Welsh)*

Key

A forward slash (/) indicates an interruption or cutoff in speech.

An ellipsis (. . .) indicates a search or trail off of thought.

The text has by and large been punctuated to serve the speech patterns of the characters and not grammatical convention.

Music

Music should play from the moment **Lisa** *turns on the stereo. We would recommend that the choice of music should aid the action and mood.*

Scene One

Llangain. March. Early evening.

The living area of the Williams' family home.

It has seen better days.

Dining table, sofa, family photos, DVDs, coffee table, stereo.

On some shelves is a collection of things that **Huw** *and his father have gathered from the coast – an hourglass, a bunch of keys, a raven's feather, a small toy London bus and at least two shells.*

One exit leads to the kitchen and the rest of the house. The other exit, the 'back door', is visible to the audience.

Dusk sunlight streams through a window; the other lights in the room are switched off.

We can hear some light evening bird song.

Huw *is cleaning the coastal objects, finishing with the hourglass.*

Tranquillity . . .

Then a noise from outside. **Huw** *looks out of the window, runs his hands through his hair, places the hourglass back onto the shelf and darts upstairs, leaving his laptop.*

Elin *opens the door, turns on the lights, takes off her coat and scans the room.*

Thomas, *outside, looks up at the sky.*

Thomas Looks like we just missed rain.

Elin That'll be a first.

Thomas *enters, shutting the door behind him.*

They look at each other.

Beat.

Elin So . . . this is it.

Thomas . . . Nice.

Elin (*unsure*) Yeah . . .

Thomas It is /

Elin I'll get us some drink. Continue this . . . this 'booze cruise'.

Elin *pushes past* **Thomas** *locking the door.*

Elin Make yourself at home.

Elin *exits.*

Thomas, *alone, takes in the space; inspecting the DVDs etc.*

Elin *enters with a bottle and two glasses.*

Elin So this is all we got.

Thomas What is it?

Elin . . . Eggnog.

Thomas (*laughs*) Great . . .

Elin I know right?

Thomas Christmas in March now is it?

Elin You gunna take your coat off or . . . ?

Elin *opens the eggnog and pours two glasses.* **Thomas** *takes his coat off revealing an adventurous choice of shirt in either colour or pattern.*

Elin (*referencing his shirt*) There it is!

Thomas Noticed did ya?

Elin Hard to miss it. Caused quite a few looks.

Thomas Did it?

Elin / A few raised eyebrows. Those poor old buggers didn't know what hit them. They went for a quiet drink and /

Elin *sophisticatedly hands* **Thomas** *a glass.*

Elin Merry Christmas Mr Stevenson.

Thomas (*laughs*) Merry Christmas Miss Williams.

Elin Call me Elin, please.

Thomas Cheers.

They drink. **Elin** *tries to play it cool then –*

Elin Fuck /

Thomas Yeah /

Elin / that's rank.

Thomas Wouldn't have been my first choice.

Elin No?

Thomas . . . More of a mulled wine man.

Elin Mulled cider is where it's at mate.

Thomas *hears something coming from upstairs.*

Thomas You hear that?

Elin What?

Thomas That noise.

Elin Pipes, I expect.

Thomas Right . . . /

Elin Old house. You know what it's like, creaks a bit.

Thomas Just /

Elin Don't worry /

Thomas I wasn't /

Elin It's just the two of us.

Thomas I /

Elin They're always at work till late.

Thomas Right.

What does your dad / do?

Elin *pulls out a packet of cigarettes and sits down on the sofa.* **Thomas** *follows.*

Elin Smoke?

Thomas . . . No.

Elin Sure?

Thomas Yeah . . .

Elin Just, 'cause, you used to.

Thomas What? /

Elin I remember seeing you, crossing the road hiding behind those cul-de-sacs puffing away /

Thomas Shit /

Elin / You weren't that discreet.

Thomas Busted!

Elin So go on then.

Thomas No thanks.

Elin No?

Thomas No.

Elin Why?

Thomas Well I . . . I quit.

Elin Quit?

Thomas Yeah /

Elin You know, the number of people that actually die from smoking, is a lot less than you'd think.

Thomas Is it?

Elin Yep.

Thomas Where'd you read that /

Elin *lights up.*

Elin Go on have one.

Thomas No /

Elin Treat yourself.

Thomas No /

Elin I won't tell if you won't /

Thomas I made myself a promise.

Elin Promise?

Thomas That I'd . . . start looking after myself /

Elin Looking after yourself?

Thomas Yeah.

Elin But . . . you've just downed three pints.

Thomas Well /

Elin On a school night.

Thomas I /

Elin Doesn't seem like you're doing a very good job.

Thomas Actually I've, I've shifted two stone.

Elin Have you?

Thomas Started hitting the gym.

Elin Oh yeah?

Thomas You should feel my tum.

Elin You offering or? /

Thomas It's firm.

Elin (*sarcastic*) Nice . . .

Thomas Now there's no need for that.

Elin What?

Thomas You know.

Elin No . . . /

Thomas Being all sarcy.

Elin I wasn't being sarcy.

Thomas Weren't ya?

Elin No!

Thomas Well there we are then.

Beat.

As they drink **Thomas** *looks* **Elin** *in the eye. Having remembered something* **Elin** *starts to laugh.*

Thomas What?

What? What's funny?

Elin Nothing . . .

Thomas No go on.

Elin Just . . . No.

Thomas Go on.

Elin No /

Thomas Don't be a killjoy.

Elin I'm not being a /

Thomas You are!

Elin Just . . . when we were at school me and a couple of the girls we, we played this game right, where we'd . . . we'd take whatever it was we were eating and, and challenge each other to eat it seductively . . .

Thomas Right . . .

Elin / like we were having dinner with you.

Thomas With me?

Elin It wasn't my idea.

Thomas Sure . . .

Elin I just . . . just played along.

Thomas Yeah right /

Elin Patrice Davies was the brains.

Thomas Who? /

Elin You know, glasses, curly hair, face like she sucked lemons /

Thomas Ostrich?

Elin What?

Thomas That's what we used to call her.

Elin Who did?

Thomas Everyone.

Elin You telling me the staff gave us nicknames?

Thomas What d'you think we'd do at lunch, sit there and play Candy Crush?

Elin I dunno talk about /

What was my nickname?

Thomas Can't remember.

Elin Yeah you can.

Thomas Can't. Promise. And even if I did I wouldn't tell ya. 'What's said in the staff room, stays in the staff room.'

Elin Now who's being a killjoy?

Beat.

Elin (*edging closer to* **Thomas**) So . . . /

Thomas Still love the coast then?

Elin What?

Thomas *points out the shells.*

Elin Oh those?

Thomas Yeah . . . /

Elin Yeah they're not mine /

Thomas No?

Elin No. My dad and brother collect things /

Thomas Right.

Elin Stuff they find. Mum likes to keep them out but /

Thomas So you're all obsessed then?

Elin Wha?

Thomas Just . . . just you used to go on about it all the time.

Elin (*slight embarrassment*) No I never?

Thomas Trust me.

Elin I didn't /

Thomas (*impersonating*) 'Mr Stevenson you must head down to Pembrey.'

Elin Fuck off.

Thomas (*impersonating*) 'You have to go when the tide is out' /

Elin Stop it.

Thomas / 'the indents left on the sand are' /

Elin *leans over and covers* **Thomas'** *mouth with her hand.*

Elin Shut up!

Elin *peels her hand away.*

Thomas I still need to find those secret spots you were always banging on about.

Elin Oh yeah?

Thomas Yeah, didn't find them last time.

Elin Well they're, they're hard to find.

Thomas Well then, whilst you're back, you'll just have to show me?

Elin Maybe . . . if I have time.

There . . . there is this spot in Llansteffan you'll like. It's just on your way up to the castle. It's dead easy to miss, you, you have to go off road, it's really fucking dangerous but, let me show you /

Elin *looks for a picture on her phone.*

Elin Here.

Elin *hands her phone to* **Thomas.**

Elin See how a bit of the cliff overhangs right, protrudes into the sea?

Thomas Yeah /

Elin I like to sit there sometimes. Smoke. Drink. Think. Look at my feet. The waves crashing against the rocks. The birds.

It's my favourite place that . . . sitting there . . . it feels like I'm sitting on the edge of the world with no one else around . . . no worries, no . . .

(*Registering what she's just said.*) Fuck . . . I think I might be a bit pissed!

Elin *jumps up and moves away.*

Thomas You look sad.

Elin Sad?

Thomas Yeah.

Elin Well it's just . . . /

Thomas What?

Elin I dunno I guess . . . /

Wanting to return to their flirtatious game **Elin** *jumps back onto the sofa.*

Elin Anyway you are the last person that can make fun of me for always talking about the coast /

Thomas Wha? /

Elin You were always banging on about London!

Thomas I /

Elin Like a broken record. Made my ears bleed.

Thomas Fuck off /

Elin Always banging on about how it's 'such a great city' /

Thomas It is!

Elin I'm not denying it!

Thomas Stop making fun then.

Elin He can give, but he can't take. Classic bloke.

Thomas You listened to me though didn't you?

Elin Well /

Thomas You with your fancy little job.

Elin I /

Thomas You went to see for yourself.

Elin Suppose.

Thomas And I was right wasn't I?

Elin . . . Maybe.

Huw *enters, unnoticed, to retrieve his laptop from the dining table.*

Thomas Come on. Walking over Waterloo Bridge, that feeling you can be anything you want. You don't get that in Carmarthen.

Elin True.

Thomas Exactly.

Elin So . . . so what brought you back then? Bar the obvious.

Thomas Obvious?

Elin *winks at* **Thomas**.

Thomas Right . . .

Elin Sussed you straight away mate.

Thomas My dad died.

Beat.

Elin Oh.

I'm /

Thomas It's alright. You weren't to know.

Elin Fuck . . .

Thomas It's fine.

Beat.

Thomas He came down to live with me. In London. When he was . . .

After he'd gone I just . . . just needed a change of scenery you know.

Elin Yeah.

Thomas And I loved it here when I was training so . . . when the job came up it, it made sense.

Huw *exits.*

Beat.

Elin So, now what? Is there a . . . is there a Mrs Stevenson?

Thomas A Mrs Stevenson?

Elin Yeah?

Thomas What do you think?

Elin What do I think? I think if I was her then I'd keep you on a tight leash.

Thomas Why is that?

Elin 'Cause I know what girls are like.

Thomas Spending their lunchtime eating seductively apparently.

Elin That was a one-time thing.

Couple of times type thing.

You have to practice!

Elin *goes in for a kiss. It's slow and passionate.* **Thomas** *breaks away.*

Thomas I can't . . .

Elin (*still flirty*) Why not?

Thomas Because I'd . . . I'd like to / do it properly.

Elin There's no one here.

Elin *goes in for another kiss. Things get more heated and passionate as they tug at each other's clothes.* **Elin** *begins to unzip* **Thomas'** *trousers but is interrupted by*

A key in the lock.

Elin *and* **Thomas** *break away just in time.* **Lisa** *opens the back door and enters, still processing the news she has received. She is carrying a shopping bag that contains some of Mr Williams' clothes.*

Elin Mum!

Lisa Elin?

Elin Why are you /

Thomas *gets up from the sofa.*

Thomas Hello.

Beat.

Elin This is /

Thomas Thomas.

Lisa Thomas?

Thomas Yes.

Lisa But /

Elin I . . .

Lisa What?

Elin I . . . I just popped into the Poplars for a quick drink /

Lisa The Poplars?

Elin Yes.

Lisa On a / weeknight?

Elin And, and, and as I was leaving, I, I bumped into . . . /

/ He was a student teacher when I was at school.

Thomas I taught her when /

Elin / When I was doing my A levels.

Thomas That's right.

Elin So we umm, we got a quick drink, you know for old times sake and then I . . . well I invited him back here for . . .

Thomas For . . .

Elin For . . .

Thomas Dinner.

Elin Dinner?

Lisa Dinner?

Thomas Yep. Elin was telling me what a wonderful cook you are.

Lisa Were you?

Elin I /

Thomas Yep . . .

Beat.

Elin Where's Huw?

Lisa What?

Elin Huw, where is he?

Lisa . . . Upstairs I imagine /

Elin Upstairs?

Thomas / Oh Jesus . . . /

Lisa He wasn't feeling well so /

Elin You mean he's been upstairs this whole time?

Lisa Well it's not like him to go out, is it?

(*Shouting up to* **Huw**.) Huw! Huw love, come down here.

He'll be up there playing one of those games of his, you know what he's like. Anyway I . . . I . . .

(*To* **Elin**.) Get the washing in will you, it's starting to spit.

Lisa *exits.*

Elin Fuck.

Thomas I mean /

Elin That was close.

Thomas My trousers were practically / falling . . .

Elin But why did you say I invited you for dinner?

Thomas I . . . I dunno /

Elin You dunno? /

Thomas I panicked.

Elin Panicked?

Thomas Yeah.

Elin Oh god.

Thomas What?

Elin Just . . .

Thomas It'll be fine /

Elin It won't /

Thomas You worry too much /

Elin You don't under / stand

Thomas Just think of all the seductive eating you'll get to do.

Elin What?

Thomas It'll be fun.

Elin You don't get it, do you?

Thomas What?

Elin Mum, she's a . . .

Thomas What?

Elin Monster.

Lisa *enters carrying a tablecloth, placemats and napkins.*

Lisa Elin. Washing!

Elin But /

Lisa Before it starts to pour.

Elin *exits through to the kitchen mouthing 'sorry' at* **Thomas** *as she leaves.*

Silence.

Thomas What's she like eh?

Beat.

Thomas Must be nice to have her back for a bit?

Lisa Who?

Thomas Elin.

Lisa Oh. Yes . . .

Silence.

Thomas I noticed you like classic films?

Lisa Sorry?

Thomas Just, noticed them earlier.

Lisa Oh those?

Thomas You must have quite a knowledge.

Lisa They're not mine.

Thomas No?

Lisa They belong to my husband.

Thomas Right . . .

Lisa I mean . . . I mean don't mind them you know I, I can 'appreciate' them /

Thomas Right /

Lisa Just, don't love them artistically like he does.

Thomas I see.

Lisa For me it was more about the men you know, Clark Gable, Humphrey Bogart, Cary Grant.

Thomas Real men?

Lisa . . . Yes . . .

Beat.

Elin *enters and exits out the back door with a basket for the washing.*

Lisa Joan Crawford I liked mind.

Thomas Yes she's . . . well she's /

Lisa What's that one where her daughter hates her?

Thomas Mildred Pierce?

Lisa That's it.

'Personally, I think alligators have the right idea.

Lisa & Thomas They eat their young.'

They laugh.

Beat.

Lisa *begins to set the table.*

Lisa Some . . . some used to say that I had a bit of the Joan Crawford about me when I was young.

Thomas Oh yeah?

Lisa Yeah . . . yeah, there's no need to be so surprised.

Thomas I . . . /

Lisa *smiles at* **Thomas** *(it's a joke). She then travels to the family photos and picks out a picture, handing it to him.*

Lisa There's me in the centre with the hair. I know? A proper 80s do. What went wrong, eh?

Thomas I can see the resemblance to /

Lisa / Crawford?

Thomas Yes . . .

Lisa *returns to setting the table.*

Thomas Where was this taken?

Lisa London.

Thomas Right /

Lisa At a gig.

Thomas Nice.

Remember who was playing?

Lisa No.

Thomas Shame.

Lisa The place was called 'The Unicorn' though, I remember that much.

Not really a name you forget.

Thomas Wonder if it's still there?

Lisa Doubt it.

Beat.

Thomas So you . . . did you live in London or were you just /

Lisa Oh no I lived there.

Thomas Nice /

Lisa Quite a few years actually.

Thomas Probably why Elin ended up there. You talking about it all the time.

Lisa Probably . . .

Thomas Why did you leave? If you don't mind me asking?

Lisa I . . . I got married I guess.

Thomas Right.

Lisa Yes.

Beat.

Lisa Actually it was . . . it was at that gig that I . . . that I met him, my husband.

Thomas Oh /

Lisa Yes /

Thomas That's /

Lisa Yes . . .

Beat.

Lisa I remember I . . . I remember this man walking through the door.

Tall. Dark. Good coat.

He caught my eye instantly. Those eyes, his eyes they . . .

Elin *enters with a full basket of washing and exits via the kitchen.*

Lisa He was softly handsome. Not immediately good looking, he wasn't one of those men. His good looks became evident through his kindness, his gentleness. Which is rare in a man isn't it? An ability to be gentle.

Thomas Yes . . .

Lisa After the gig he, he approached me and we just . . . well we hit it off straight away.

Thomas And why was that do you think?

Lisa Well because . . . I think it was because he was older than me /

Thomas Right /

Lisa Yes. Meant he knew who he was . . .

It was sad in a way, leaving London, stop being Lisa Llewellyn but . . . but that's one of the benefits of marriage isn't it? Allows a woman to become someone else. Someone new.

Anyway, enough about me.

Thomas It's fine.

Lisa *replaces the photo and gently adjusts the position of the hourglass.*

Thomas Will he be joining us?

Lisa Who?

Thomas Your husband?

Lisa . . . No /

Thomas No? /

Lisa Not tonight.

Thomas Right.

Lisa *goes to the back door and locks it.*

Thomas Working late is he?

Lisa No.

Thomas No?

Lisa He's away.

Thomas Oh.

Anywhere nice?

Lisa He'll be back soon /

Thomas Right /

Lisa But, but tonight it's just me you Elin and Huw.

Beat.

Thomas Well . . . it'll be nice to meet him.

Lisa Who?

Thomas Huw. Elin's been talking about him.

Lisa Was she?

Thomas 'Bout his collection /

Lisa My husband's collection.

Thomas / Seems really interesting . . .

Lisa Well yes he's . . . well he's . . .

Thomas It'll be really nice to meet him.

The penny-drops. **Lisa** *looks at* **Thomas**, *he smiles.*

Lisa Oh.

Oh.

Oh god.

As if seeing **Thomas** *properly for the first time.*

Lisa (*under her breath*) How stupid.

Beat.

Thomas . . . are you alright?

Lisa Me?

Yes. I'm . . . I'm fine. Just . . .

. . . just

. . . just the house is an absolute state.

Lisa *starts tidying up. She travels to the front door and makes sure it's locked.*

Thomas Oh it's /

Lisa I had no idea that you were . . .

Thomas Don't worry /

Lisa It's just /

Thomas No need to /

Lisa Elin didn't give me any warning /

Thomas I'm not fussy /

Lisa I wasn't ready for /

Thomas Really it's /

Lisa Has Elin been smoking in here?

Thomas Urm /

Lisa The number of times I've had to tell her. It affects Huw's asthma.

Lisa *gets out an air freshener and gives it a spray. As she does this she knocks into* **Thomas** *causing him to spill his drink on himself.*

Lisa Oh I!

I am so, so, sorry. /

Thomas It's fine.

Lisa *grabs a napkin.* **Elin** *enters.*

Lisa Let me just.

Thomas I /

Lisa *dabs* **Thomas**, *able to feel his muscles.*

Elin Mum? /

Lisa (*under her breath*) Oh god!

Thomas I think /

Lisa You, you have to attack the moisture straight away.

Thomas Right.

Lisa Otherwise you've got no chance.

Lisa *pulls away to inspect* **Thomas'** *shirt.*

Thomas Honestly, it's /

Lisa That might stain.

Thomas D'ya think? /

Lisa Know what I'll do? Know what'll do it?

Quick wash.

Thomas What? /

Elin / No /

Lisa We get it in the wash straight away, there's less of a chance it'll stain.

Thomas But /

Elin / Mum /

Lisa I'll just go and fetch you a spare.

Lisa *exits.*

Elin Fuck.

Thomas It's fine.

Elin I'm sorry /

Thomas Don't worry about /

Elin You better be off before she chucks something else on you.

Thomas Nah you're alright, I'm enjoying myself.

Elin Wha?

Thomas You know, getting to know the in-laws.

Elin But /

Thomas She got a bit weird when I mentioned your dad but /

Elin Dad? /

Thomas But otherwise she seems fun.

Beat.

Elin Don't do that.

Thomas What?

Elin Encourage her.

Thomas Why? /

Elin She's a dangerous woman with an agreeable audience.

Thomas Oh come off it.

Elin I'm serious, now's your / last chance to leave.

Lisa *enters with one of Mr Williams' shirts.*

Lisa I thought you could pop this on.

Thomas Oh /

Lisa It's one of my husband's.

Elin Mum /

Lisa Nothing special. (*Pointing at* **Thomas'** *shirt.*) Not like this but, but it should do the trick.

Thomas Right well . . .

Is there a bathroom?

Lisa Just, just up the stairs first door on the left.

Thomas Cheers.

Thomas *exits.*

Lisa I'm absolutly mortified.

Elin Mum /

Lisa What was I thinking.

Elin It's /

Lisa We have somebody over /

Elin Don't / worry about

Lisa / And I throw a fucking drink over him /

Elin So obviously I invited Thomas over thinking /

Lisa I know exactly why you invited Thomas over.

Elin You do?

Lisa Yes.

Elin (*under her breath*) Fuck.

Lisa And I am delighted.

Elin What?

Lisa I was surprised when I walked through the door don't get me wrong /

Elin So was I but /

Lisa Took me a while to realise /

Elin Did it?

Lisa It wasn't until I was talking to him, just the two of us.

Elin Right /

Lisa But you . . . you seem to have done a good job so far.

Elin You think?

Lisa Baited him. Hooked him. Reeled him in. And what a catch he is I tell you. Polite, charming; even easy on the eye.

Elin Well I /

Lisa Could have given us a little bit of warning though.

Elin But I /

Lisa I mean the house is an absolute state. I wasn't ready for him. Keep an ear out for the flush.

So, come on, quickly, give us the goss? What do you know?

Elin Well I . . . I dunno.

Lisa Where in town is he living?

Elin Didn't ask.

Lisa Typical /

Elin Walking distance to the school though I imagine.

Lisa Johnstown maybe?

Elin Maybe.

Lisa Could be worse, could be Park Hall.

Elin And he's, he's Head of Geography now. Head of department. I guess that's something.

Lisa Something! He must be what early thirties? /

Elin / Yeah /

Lisa That takes something to become a head of a department that young I can tell you. No, no, no this is good. This proves he has drive, charisma.

Elin I /

Lisa / Now then, you collected the washing?

Elin Yes /

Lisa I'll finish setting the table, and we'll, we'll have a few bottles of wine over supper. High-percentage reds, you know? Loosen us up.

Elin We're out.

Lisa What?

Elin Of wine.

Lisa What happened to them?

Elin Someone drunk them I imagine.

Lisa More like you drunk them.

Elin I /

Lisa Because that's what you do isn't it?

Elin Mum /

Lisa Bloody typical.

Elin We have the eggnog.

Lisa What?

Elin This. (*Showing her the bottle.*)

Lisa You've been drinking that?

Elin Yeah.

Lisa Why?

Elin It's all I could find.

Lisa Oh there we are then. Invite a man over, a man with a little bit of class, oh I know what I'll give him, a bottle of eggnog from about nine Christmases ago.

Elin He didn't mind!

Lisa Forgot about the total option of just popping out and buying something else, did you? He's probably up there now, sitting on the toilet, frothing at the mouth.

Elin I'll go out and get some.

Elin *goes to leave.*

Lisa Wait . . . take him with you.

Elin Wha?

Lisa Take him with you to the shop.

Elin Why?

Lisa It'll give me time to . . . to sort this place out.

Elin But /

Lisa Shush now. I can hear him.

Thomas *enters wearing Mr Williams' shirt, carrying his own.*

Thomas (*referencing his shirt*) Cheers for this.

Mr Williams likes labelling his clothes does he?

Beat.

Lisa It looks lovely on you. Don't you think Elin? Fits you like a glove, love.

Lisa *takes* **Thomas'** *shirt.*

Thomas Think I got most of it off.

Lisa (*inspecting the shirt*) Looks like you have but, but I'll just put it through a quick wash. Better to be safe than be sorry . . . and you never know with 'eggnog'.

Lisa *exits with the shirt.*

Elin Nice.

Thomas I think I make it work.

Elin Let's not get too carried away.

Thomas So what were you two gossiping about?

Elin Oh . . . stuff.

Thomas Stuff?

Elin Yeah . . .

Thomas Like?

Elin Like I need to fetch some wine, if you want to come with? Make a night of it.

Thomas You've changed your tune.

Elin Have I?

Thomas You were practically begging me to leave a moment ago.

Elin Well you're . . . you're right . . . it might be fun.

Elin *gives him a quick kiss. Then goes to grab her coat.* **Thomas** *looks out of the window.*

Thomas Rain's stopped.

Elin For now, yeah. You're in Wales remember.

Elin *throws his coat at him.* **Lisa** *enters.*

Lisa Going somewhere?

Elin We're um . . . just popping out to get some wine.

Lisa Well, don't be long.

Elin *and* **Thomas** *exit out the back door. As soon as they've left* **Lisa** *automatically turns the key.*

Scene Two

Twenty-five minutes have passed since **Thomas** *and* **Elin** *exited.*

The action picks up with **Lisa** *mid-conversation as she sets the dining table.* **Huw** *is holding the plates, cutlery, candles etc. while his laptop sits open on the coffee table.*

Lisa / So me and Elin, we had this idea, well it was more my idea but, to help you you know, 'find someone'.

Huw Find someone? /

Lisa / 'Cause it's not easy these days is it, especially round here, your options really are limited to . . . oh what's Helen Creamer's boy called?

Huw Kieran.

Lisa That's the one, and you are far better than that.

Huw Mhm /

Lisa Anyway we thought, well I thought, because you are, you know . . . /

Huw What?

Lisa Quiet, and I figured that Elin might know the odd . . .

Huw The odd?

Lisa You know . . . /

Huw Quiet? /

Lisa So basically I asked her to keep an eye out.

Huw For what?

Lisa / If I'm honest I was beginning to think she wasn't even trying. First couple of days I thought 'fair enough' I know Carmarthen isn't a gay hotspot. /

Huw No /

Lisa But after being back a few weeks I was thinking 'surely she'd have thought of someone by now'.

Huw But Mum /

Lisa And yet still nothing. But tonight, tonight, out of nowhere, she has pulled a corker out the bag. And I'm telling you something love he was worth the wait.

Huw What /

Lisa Just the type of man you need.

Huw I /

Lisa Smart, polite, cultured. Lover of classic films, just like your father.

Huw I'm not looking for someone who likes /

Lisa No, no, no, I think you two are going to get on like a house on fire.

Huw I can't / believe this.

Lisa You're surprised aren't you?

Huw What / ?

Lisa I have to admit I was surprised too, what with Elin being so /

Huw No it's /

Lisa But you know, I think, inevitably, she knows it's all you want.

Huw But /

Lisa No idea what she's said to him love, but whatever it is, he's very excited to talk to you.

Huw Oh god /

Lisa Now there's no need to worry /

Huw I can't . . .

Lisa What do you mean you can't?

Huw I can't.

Lisa You can and you will.

Huw But I don't want to.

Lisa Yes you do!

Huw No I don't.

Lisa Elin has invited Thomas over /

Huw But Mum I can't.

Lisa Don't be daft, of course you can /

Huw No /

Lisa Don't be so /

Huw You don't understand.

Lisa What?

Huw He used to teach me.

Lisa Teach you?

Huw Yes!

Lisa And that's a problem because?

Huw / Because . . . /

Lisa / Because?

Huw I just can't /

Lisa Why is that a problem?

Huw Well he was . . . he was kind, he was nice, he . . . he actually paid me some attention and . . .

Lisa And?

Huw . . . and as a result . . .

Lisa Christ speak up!

Lisa *abandons setting the table.*

Huw Oh Mum I just can't.

Lisa As a result what?

Huw Well . . . /

Lisa Come on /

Huw I guess I had a crush on him.

Beat.

Lisa That's fantastic.

Huw No, that's not fanta / stic

Lisa I actually thought something was the matter for a moment.

Huw What /

Lisa That for once something was 'actually' wrong. /

Huw Something is actually wrong /

Lisa Like he'd had some sort of illicit affair with a friend of yours or something.

Huw You don't understand /

Lisa Oh I understand love don't you worry. I was young once /

Huw I know but /

Lisa There was a boy at my school right, David Davies, who I had the biggest crush on /

Huw I don't need to hear this /

Lisa / Crippling crush. Couldn't string a sentence in his presence type of crush /

Huw / It's not the same as /

Lisa / We sat next to each other once on a school trip to Aberystwyth and the sexual tension was palpable.

Huw Oh Christ /

Lisa / The only thing about David was he suffered from travel sickness /

Huw It's worse than that.

Lisa How?

Huw Because I . . . I, I kind of became obsessed with him.

Lisa Obsessed?

Huw Yeah like . . .

Lisa Like?

Huw Like I'd follow him home after school. Knew who his friends were. Where he lived. What car he drove, I . . . oh God.

Lisa Did he know?

Huw No I . . . I dunno.

Lisa There we are then love. It's fine to follow people around, so long as you don't get caught.

Lisa *continues setting the table.*

Huw (*running his hands through his hair*) And he gave me a nickname.

Beat.

Lisa A nickname?

Huw Yes?

Lisa What nickname?

Huw I . . . can't remember.

Lisa Yes you can.

Huw I /

Lisa What nickname?

Huw He called me Glas.

Beat.

Lisa Glas?

Huw Yes.

Lisa Because you're fragile?

Huw No.

Lisa No? /

Huw It's the Welsh word for blue.

Lisa Right /

Huw Because I was always off sick.

Lisa 'Feeling blue' /

Huw Yes.

Lisa Smart.

Huw And it rhymes with /

Lisa This is excellent news love /

Huw What /

Lisa / This, is a 'game changer'.

Huw No /

Lisa He gave you a nickname.

Huw Yeah but /

Lisa People don't go around giving people nicknames unless they want them.

Huw What?

Lisa Just think of your father?

Huw Mum /

Lisa All those nicknames he has for me.

Huw I don't /

Lisa 'Cariad. Cloncen.'

Huw But this is /

Lisa / no idea what half of them mean but it doesn't matter /

Huw But I don't /

Lisa And look at you. You've really blossomed into something quite unique.

Huw I haven't blossomed into anything /

Lisa Stop putting yourself down.

Huw But /

Lisa / Any man would be lucky to have you /

Huw I /

Lisa / But I won't let you go for any man.

Huw Thank you / but

Lisa / But this one, this one's a winner.

Huw A winner?

Lisa All you've got to do is talk to him love.

Huw I can't.

Lisa Of course you can.

Huw But . . . but he won't remember me.

Lisa Of course he will /

Huw No /

Lisa You're impossible to forget.

Huw But /

Lisa*'s focus returns to* **Huw**.

Lisa What did we agree?

Huw Mum /

Lisa What did we agree now that Dad's . . . /

Huw That I'd . . . that I'd try and /

Lisa / Find someone?

Huw But I / can't

Lisa Because we have been waiting for this moment /

Huw But /

Lisa Because I can't do it on my own /

Huw Mum /

Lisa I'm not as strong as I look /

Huw That's not /

Lisa And now with your father's funding /

Huw / Funding? /

Lisa My wage isn't enough to keep us afloat.

Huw But what do you /

Lisa He's not getting any money.

Beat.

Huw What?

Lisa They told me earlier when I went to see him.

Huw But /

Lisa Apparently, according to the state, he 'earned too much'.

Huw But that's not /

Lisa So instead, instead they are going to take everything from us. The house. His savings. Everything he worked for. Everything he left for you, until there is absolutely nothing left.

Huw But /

Lisa I don't worry about your sister. I know she'll be alright. But you? You need somebody love.

Huw No I / don't.

Lisa You do. You need somebody just like I need somebody.

Huw But /

Lisa A good man, with a good job, who'll be able to give you what I've been giving you, so don't, for goodness sake, throw this opportunity away.

Huw But /

Lisa All you've got to do is try love. That's all you've got to do. That's all I'm asking!

Beat.

Huw Fine.

Silence.

Lisa *returns to the table.*

Huw What do I talk about?

Lisa Oh just . . . just . . . you know . . .

Huw Just?

Lisa Well, anything?

Huw Anything?

Lisa Yes, you know . . . I don't know . . . work?

Huw Work?

Lisa Yes . . . just . . .

Huw Oh God . . .

Lisa Now don't worry love /

Huw But I . . . I don't know what to / talk about.

Lisa Something will come in the moment.

Huw No it won't.

Lisa Yes it will.

Beat.

(*Remembering.*) He's head of department now.

Huw What?

Lisa Elin was telling me earlier, Head of Geography.

Huw OK . . .

Lisa There you go, ask him about that. 'I've heard you are Head of Geography now, that's fantastic'. That'll get the ball rolling. Men love talking about their successes.

Huw I guess.

Lisa Mention that and he'll be off on one.

Huw OK.

Lisa You'll be a natural, just like your mother.

Lisa *inspects the table.*

Lisa Go and fetch some wine glasses from the kitchen will you.

Huw *goes to exit.*

Lisa Four.

Huw Four?

Lisa Yes.

Huw But /

Lisa There will be wine at the table and you will have a glass.

Huw But /

Lisa We can't have a guest over, open a bottle of wine, and have you sitting there drinking a Vimto.

Huw It always upsets my /

Lisa / it'll grow on you, you just have to try it a few times.

Huw But /

Lisa You are having a glass of wine with supper and that's final.

Huw Fine . . .

Huw *exits.*

Lisa *lights candles and turns on lamps, to give the room a more romantic atmosphere.*

She selects some CDs and puts them into the system. The volume is gentle and not too overpowering.

She gently adjusts some of the coastal objects.

Huw *enters with four wine glasses, setting them on the table.*

Lisa There's a good boy. Wasn't so difficult was it?

Huw I guess not.

Lisa (*presenting the space*) What do you think?

Huw Uhh . . .

Lisa We've had very little time but I think, I think there's some romance don't you?

Huw Yeah . . .

Lisa Right, now then, we better get changed.

Huw Changed?

Lisa We can't have dinner dressed like this.

Huw Why not?

Lisa Well it's . . . it's not very flattering is it?

Huw Flattering?

Lisa I mean look at your jumper /

Huw What about it?

Lisa Well it's . . . it's all baggy /

Huw Oh /

Lisa And there's holes in the sleeves. No, no, no tell you what, why don't you put on that nice blue one I bought you.

Huw But /

Lisa The tight one. The one I bought you for /

Elin *and* **Thomas** *are outside, trying to open the back door.*

Elin Mum. Mum! Let us in.

(*To* **Thomas**.) She's got this terrible habit of locking it.

(*Knocking harder.*) MUM!

Lisa Well go on love. Welcome him in.

Huw But /

Huw *looks at* **Lisa** *reluctantly. She gestures for him to open the door. He does it tentatively.* **Elin** *rushes in pushing* **Huw** *aside.* **Thomas** *hangs by the door.*

Elin Finally. It's fucking freezing out there.

Lisa Language Elin.

Elin Well it is.

Elin *takes her coat off and puts down the bottles of wine before registering the room's different atmosphere.*

Elin Why have you . . . ?

Lisa We thought we'd . . . create a little bit of atmosphere /

Elin But /

Lisa Didn't we love?

Huw Yeah /

Elin Why? /

Lisa Set the scene, so to speak.

Elin *shrugs this off and starts to open one of the bottles.*
Thomas *enters.*

Elin (*to* **Thomas**) So anyway, Bertie was spread eagled on the boss's desk, right /

Lisa Elin /

Elin And then the police turned up.

Thomas Shit /

Lisa Elin /

Elin But by that time it was too late 'cause /

Lisa Elin!

Elin What?

Lisa Will you go and check on the food?

Elin Can't you?

Lisa No.

Elin Why?

Lisa Because . . . I need to get changed.

Elin Changed?

Lisa Put on something a little more . . . flattering.

Elin Why?

Lisa Because . . . just go and do it please.

Elin But /

Lisa Please.

Elin Fine.

Lisa Great, well, I won't be a moment.

As **Lisa** *exits she locks the back door and pockets the key before noticing* **Elin** *hasn't moved.*

Lisa Elin!

Elin Coming.

Lisa *exits.*

Elin Open a bottle and get cosy. I might be a while.

Elin *exits with the open bottle.*

Thomas *and* **Huw** *are alone.*

Thomas (*he laughs*) She's nuts.

Silence.

Feeling uncomfortable in his clothes **Huw** *pulls at his jumper, trying to make himself more presentable.* **Thomas** *smiles at* **Huw**. **Huw** *looks to his laptop.*

Thomas What's that?

Huw . . . A game.

Thomas Mint.

What game?

Huw . . . Minecraft.

Thomas Nice.

Huw You know it?

Thomas No.

Huw Oh.

Beat.

Thomas I've heard of it though. Lot of my students play it . . . friends.

Huw Nice /

Thomas Just I haven't /

Huw No.

Thomas Not yet anyway.

Huw Would you like to?

Thomas What?

Huw Play?

Thomas Oh.

Maybe later.

Huw OK.

Thomas *smiles.*

Huw It's my favourite.

Thomas Is it?

Huw Yeah . . .

Thomas . . . Why?

Huw Dunno.

Thomas Oh.

Huw I guess . . . I guess the game play is only restricted by the limit of your imagination.

Thomas Right /

Huw So it means like, anything is possible.

Thomas The possibilities are endless?

Huw Yeah . . .

Thomas Nice /

Huw But you can only really go as far as your imagination will let you.

Thomas Which is endless.

Huw I guess.

Beat.

Huw And it's not violent.

Thomas Makes a change.

Huw Yeah. Mum wouldn't, when I was little, let me play violent games.

Thomas Makes sense.

Huw And now I don't like them.

Thomas Well that's good.

Huw Yeah.

Silence.

Then, after a while **Huw** *remembers . . .*

Huw (*sounding slightly prepared*) I've heard you are Head of Geography now? That's fantastic.

Thomas Oh thanks yeah it's . . . it is pretty exciting.

Beat.

Huw Enjoying?

Thomas What? /

Huw Your job?

Thomas Yes . . . so far anyway.

Huw Cool . . .

Thomas Not that we're meant to enjoy what we do.

Huw No.

/ I mean /

Thomas / Different now though, being head of department.

Huw I bet.

Thomas People treat me differently.

Huw Yeah /

Thomas Offer me a little bit more respect.

Huw Nice.

Thomas Sure Elin would still be a nightmare to teach mind.

Huw Would she? /

Thomas (*almost whispering*) We used to call her 'Motor' in the staff room.

Huw Right.

Why?

Thomas Well because . . .

Huw (*understanding*) Oh.

Thomas Yeah.

Huw Because she could drive.

Thomas No.

Huw No?

Thomas No. Motormouth.

Huw Oh /

Thomas But don't tell her that. That'll be our little secret.

Huw Oh, OK.

Beat.

Huw People are often giving people nicknames at school aren't they?

Thomas Yeah, suppose so.

Beat.

Huw *looks at* **Thomas**, *trying to jog his memory.* **Thomas**' *attention returns to* **Huw**'s *laptop.*

Thomas So is this one of those you play with mates?

Huw No.

Thomas No?

Huw I mean, you can if you want but . . . I tend to . . . on my own.

Thomas Right.

Huw I do have friends though, online.

Thomas Yeah?

Huw Yeah, I'm a member of a forum.

Thomas 'Bout Minecraft?

Huw And other games. My best friend is Skywalker44.

Thomas Nice.

Huw His real name's James though.

Thomas Right.

Huw He lives in London.

Thomas Cool.

Huw We Skype and things. He's nice.

Beat.

Thomas (*trying out the name*) Skywalker44.

Huw Yeah.

Thomas Why's he called that?

Huw Oh I . . . I dunno . . . I . . . I guess it's a nickname.

Thomas Right.

Huw Yeah.

Beat.

Thomas Do you have a nickname?

Huw Me?

Thomas Yeah.

Huw . . . No.

Thomas No?

Huw . . . No.

Thomas What about at school?

Huw At school?

Thomas Yeah.

Beat.

Huw No . . .

Huw *runs his hands through his hair.* **Thomas** *recognises something in this.*

Thomas Wait a minute.

Glas?

Beat.

Huw Yeah.

Thomas It's you.

Huw Yeah.

Thomas Fuck!

Huw You remembered /

Thomas I . . .

I had no idea you were Elin's brother.

Huw Not a . . . not a lot of people / do

Thomas Why didn't you say something earlier?

Huw I dunno I /

Thomas You should have said.

Huw Sorry.

Thomas Don't apologise.

Huw I . . . I didn't think you'd remember me.

Thomas Well I . . . well I did didn't I?

Huw Yeah . . . you have a good mem / ory

Thomas Just had no idea you were Elin's brother /

Huw Well we /

Thomas Normally I make the sibling connection after about two lessons /

Huw Yeah /

Thomas / but you two clearly slipped me by.

Huw Well we're . . . we're very different I guess.

Thomas She's all mouth you mean?

Huw And I'm really shy.

Thomas Ey now, there's nothing wrong with shyness.

Huw No?

Thomas Not at all, just means your more content with who you are.

Huw I guess.

Beat.

Thomas Sorry I didn't recognise you earlier.

Huw That's alright.

Thomas Can totally see it now just /

Huw It's / fine.

Thomas You look different.

Huw Yeah . . . yeah I've really blossomed into something quite /

Thomas Wine?

Huw Uh. . .yeah.

Thomas Good lad.

Thomas *opens a bottle and pours two glasses.*

Thomas So what you up to?

Huw Oh . . . not much.

Thomas Not much?

Huw No.

Huw *takes a sip and coughs.*

Thomas Well, what have you been up to then?

Huw Been up to?

Thomas Yeah?

Huw Oh just . . . this and that.

Thomas This and that?

Huw Yeah.

Thomas Well . . . what sort of this and that?

Huw Oh you know . . .

Thomas No?

Huw Well . . . um . . . Minecraft.

Thomas Right.

Huw Yeah . . .

Thomas Anything else?

Huw Well I . . .

Thomas Work, uni /

Huw I have my stuff from the coast?

Thomas (*remembering*) Oh, yeah.

Huw Yeah . . .

Thomas What's that about?

Huw Well it's . . . it's . . . well . . . before . . . me Elin and Dad we . . . we used to spend all our weekends down there.

Thomas Used to? /

Huw Elin would go off and, and, and me and Dad would . . . we'd wander the shoreline.

Thomas Right /

Huw Yeah and . . . and every so often we'd find something, you know, washed up on the shore; something lost, something old, something broken, something in need of repair and . . . and we'd bring it back here. Bring it home and, and together we'd try and restore it to what it once was.

Like this . . .

Huw *takes the hourglass off the shelf.*

This was a great find. It's made of glass look, and, amazingly it hadn't smashed when it was lost at sea, even though it's so delicate.

Huw *hands the hourglass to* **Thomas**, *their hands briefly touching.*

Huw When I found it it was empty. The stopper had come off and it had lost its sand, so I had to replace it. Because it's sad isn't it, an hourglass that doesn't work, because it's purposeless.

Thomas What does it time?

Huw Exactly ten minutes.

Thomas Does it now?

Huw Yeah.

Thomas Shall we test that theory?

Huw You can if you want but . . . but I know that it does.

Thomas Alright then, I'll trust ya.

Huw I'm very trustworthy.

Thomas Yeah?

Huw That's what Elin's always saying.

Thomas Is she?

Huw Good at keeping secrets.

Thomas Elin's secrets?

Huw . . . I guess.

Thomas Like?

Huw Like . . .

Wait a minute if I tell you, it won't be a secret anymore would it?

Thomas Suppose not.

Thomas *puts the hourglass back on the shelf.*

Huw . . . So I also found /

Thomas What type of feather is this?

Huw A . . . /

Thomas *pulls the feather off the shelf.*

Huw A raven's I think.

Thomas Nice.

Huw Yeah /

Thomas Where did ya /

Huw My dad found it.

Thomas Right . . .

Huw Yeah . . .

Thomas Where is he by the /

Huw They've got incredible memories, ravens, apparently they can connect your face to any previous encounter.

Thomas Cool.

Huw I read it online.

Thomas Nice. But /

Huw I like birds.

Thomas Same. But where /

Huw They're free aren't they?

Thomas . . . Yes . . . yes suppose they are.

Silence.

Huw I think I'm going to give you a nickname.

Thomas Me?

Huw Yeah.

Thomas Why?

Huw Because if you /

I'm going to call you . . . Aderyn.

Thomas Aderyn?

Huw Yeah.

Thomas That's pretty.

Huw Yeah . . .

Thomas What's it mean?

Huw It means . . .

I'm not going to tell you.

Thomas No?

Huw No /

Thomas But /

Huw It's my secret.

Thomas Secret?

Huw Yeah.

Thomas Oh, go on!

Huw No.

Thomas Go on.

Huw No /

Elin *enters.*

Elin (*to* **Huw**) Will you come and give me a hand, she's made a shed load.

Thomas I'll come.

Elin/Huw No.

Thomas Really. Please. Let me help.

Thomas *exits through to the kitchen.* **Elin** *turns to follow him.*

Huw Elin?

Elin Yeah?

Huw Thank you.

Elin For what?

Huw . . . Helping . . .

Elin Don't be daft mun.

Huw I really / appreciate it.

Elin Me and you, we're in this together.

Huw Yeah . . .

He's nice by the way.

Elin D'you think?

Huw Yeah.

Elin . . . Yeah . . . yeah I think so too.

Beat.

Elin Anyway I better . . .

Huw Course.

Elin Before /

Lisa (*off*) Elin!

Elin *smiles at* **Huw**.

Lisa (*off*) Elin!

Elin Right on cue.

Lisa (*off*) Elin!

Elin Coming.

Elin *exit, leaving* **Huw** *alone. He smiles.*

Scene Three

A brief amount of time has passed.

During this time **Thomas** *and* **Elin** *have entered from the kitchen setting a stew like dish and a selection of different vegetables.* **Thomas'** *shirt is now hanging up, drying off.*

The action resumes as **Elin** *brings in the last of the food and* **Lisa** *(who is now more formally dressed) hands* **Huw** *a jumper. He quickly changes into this before going to sit in his usual seat.*

Lisa No, no, love, sit here.

Huw But that's Dad's /

Lisa You can play the man of the house.

Thomas? (*Indicating where he can sit.*)

Elin *is about to sit down when –*

Lisa Elin, you can serve.

During the following **Elin** *ladles stew seductively into* **Thomas'** *bowl.*

Lisa Now then, just so you know, everything on the table is meat free.

Thomas Great.

Elin How much / do you want?

Lisa One of those as well are you?

Thomas Urm /

Lisa Huw's all about saving the animals.

Elin Since / when

Lisa You do much cooking?

Thomas When I have the / time.

Lisa You must be very busy?

Thomas Yes /

Lisa All those reports to write, lessons to plan /

Thomas Well it's /

Lisa Good money though?

Thomas Not bad, but /

Lisa Holidays?

Thomas Yes, but /

Elin (*referencing the stew*) What's in this?

Lisa Quorn. Huw helped me make it.

Elin You know /

Lisa He's a wonderful cook aren't you love?

Huw I'm /

Elin / Quorn is actually worse for you than chicken.

Lisa What?

Elin It's true.

Lisa Don't be daft.

Elin Read it online.

Lisa Well people can write any old rubbish these days.

Elin But /

Lisa Tell you what Huw loves / making

Elin If you think about it though, if you think about it logically, it's all processed, it's not natural.

Lisa Oh here she goes again /

Elin I /

Lisa Getting on her high horse.

Elin Just making a point /

Lisa Interrupting my flow /

Elin I'm just saying that /

Lisa But when you don't eat meat there isn't much choice, is there?

Elin Actually in London, I go to veggie restaurants all the /

Thomas I think it's super.

Lisa Why thank you. Hear that Huw? He thinks it's super.

Huw Yes.

Silence.

Lisa, *silently, is trying to get* **Huw** *to speak.*

Thomas Huw was telling me about his Minecraft.

Lisa His what?

Thomas Minecraft, on the computer.

Lisa Right.

Huw Thomas wanted to know how it worked /

Lisa Did he?

Huw / Cause a lot of his friends play it, but he never had /

Lisa Great.

Huw / and I told him it was my favourite /

Lisa Good.

Elin *takes her seat to eat.*

Huw / 'cause the game play is only restricted by the limit of your imagination so it means like /

Lisa Bugger it!

Elin What?

Lisa I've forgotten the bread!

Huw So it means like /

Lisa It's still in the kitchen.

Elin I'll go.

Elin *goes to exit.*

Lisa And grab another bottle of wine will you?

Elin How many hands do you think I have?

Thomas I'll come and help.

They exit together.

Lisa What the bloody hell are you playing at?

Huw What /

Lisa There I was trying to make you sound like a good cook.

Huw But /

Lisa Giving you something to talk about /

Huw I /

Lisa And you started talking about that fucking Minecraft.

Huw I don't /

Lisa All you've got to do is talk to him love like a normal human being. You know, ask him if he wants another glass of wine, how his day was, if he has any pets, I don't know, anything, just don't talk about that bloody game.

Elin *and* **Thomas** *return.*

Silence.

Huw (*to* **Thomas**) Would you like another glass of wine?

Thomas Oh, yes please.

Lisa, *subtly, gestures at* **Huw** *to speak.* **Elin** *continues to eat seductively.*

Huw Did you have a good day?

Thomas Uh, yeah.

Same as usual really.

Huw Do you have any pets?

Thomas Pets?

Lisa Oh Huw love sit down.

Huw *sits.* **Elin** *pushes the naughtiness of the seductive eating.*

Thomas (*laughing*) Stop it!

Beat. They eat.

That's a, that's a very nice necklace Mrs Williams.

Elin What /

Lisa This?

Elin (*through gritted teeth*) Thomas! /

Lisa Oh, it was a, it was a gift from my husband /

Elin I . . . /

Lisa / he's very romantic like that.

Thomas Right /

Lisa Always giving me gifts.

Thomas Lucky you. Shame he's not here I'd /

Lisa I remember I . . . I'd spotted the box hidden in his sock draw.

Elin Mum /

Lisa Because men are awful at hiding things aren't they?

Thomas Some are but not /

Lisa It was deep purple, luxurious and large.

Elin Mum /

Lisa As soon as I saw it I wanted to peek I can tell you. But I didn't.

Elin We don't need to /

Lisa I'm not a great actress you see. If I'd have seen the necklace before he'd given it to me he would have known. Killing the moment. Killing the romance. And one should never kill the romance.

Elin Why don't we /

Huw (*to* **Elin**) Let her tell it.

Lisa That particular evening we were heading out for dinner somewhere fancy; I'd bathed, perfumed, Ella Fitzgerald was playing on the vinyl and I, I'd slipped into this little black number /

Because that's all men want really isn't it, something simple /

Because the moment you put on something elaborate they can't imagine you naked, and if they can't imagine you naked you are nothing to them /

Thomas I'm not sure that's /

Lisa / Anyway, anyway, anyway I was just finishing off my face, right, when he crept up behind me. 'Close your eyes' he said. My heart was racing by now I can tell you. A cold sweat had come over me. I was short of breath and . . .

. . . and when he put it on me it was . . . it was cold, it was heavy, it made the hairs on the back of my neck stand on end and, and when I opened my eyes I . . . I just burst into tears.

Beat.

Lisa See . . . that's the difference now /

Elin What is?

Lisa Women don't know how to dress themselves.

Thomas Well . . . /

Lisa These days they either wear too little, you know, tummy out, tits up, knickers on show, which men don't find attractive /

Thomas Sadly I think you'll find /

Lisa Well, the type of man one wants to attract. Men with a little bit of class, they want a little bit of suspense.

Thomas True, but /

Lisa Or, and Elin is the prime example, they don't dress at all.

Elin What?

Lisa They make no effort whatsoever.

Elin Cheers /

Lisa Proving that women no longer know how to properly court.

Elin I can't believe that /

Lisa That's why you have hordes of these single women right; marriages breaking down, lonely old spinsters with cats because they don't know what they're doing.

Elin (*under her breath*) Here we go /

Lisa It was different back in my day Thomas I can tell you. We knew, I knew how to win a man, what feminine qualities to employ.

As **Lisa** *begins to list her 'feminine qualities'* **Huw** *is subtly trying to copy her.*

Elin Did you now?

Lisa Of course. See, a girl like me, from Cardiff /

Elin / Ponty /

Lisa / From just outside Cardiff I had to develop a nimble wit, a good posture. I learnt how to eat slowly and gracefully at supper. I developed charm.

Because people may be gifted with beauty, /

Lisa/Huw 'But you have to earn charm.' /

Elin Oh forgodsake /

Lisa / That's my boy! You see it's like getting ready for battle. And I was ready for war.

(*To* **Elin**.) Which is what I've always been telling you love. But you've never listened have you? And now look at you.

Thomas Oh I don't / know

Lisa Whereas your brother? Well . . . he takes after his mother.

Elin Does he?

Huw Yes, yes I do.

Silence. They finish eating. **Lisa** *smiles, a job well done.* **Huw** *smiles at* **Thomas**.

Lisa Well, looks like that went down well.

Thomas It was lovely Mrs Williams.

Lisa Lisa please I insist, but Huw did most of the work.

Thomas (*to* **Huw**) Well in that case, thank you.

Elin Finished Mum? You've hardly eaten. Didn't enjoy it?

Lisa I'm watching my figure love. Some people do that.

Lisa *gets up from the table and makes her way to the shelves.*

Lisa Know what we need now?

Elin (*under her breath*) / Another drink? /

Lisa A game.

Lisa *gently adjusts the hourglass before picking up a box.*

Huw Game?

Lisa Yes love, nice little game to help get the dinner down.

Lisa *places the box on the dining table.*

Lisa Huw's excellent at this one.

Huw Am I? /

Thomas What is it?

Lisa Charades. Know it?

Thomas Uhh /

Elin (*grabbing the box*) Me first.

Lisa (*snatching the box off her*) No.

Elin Why not?

Lisa Huw first.

Elin Why?

Lisa (*trying to hint to* **Elin**) Because . . .

Elin Because?

Lisa . . . Because I said so.

(*Handing the box to* **Huw**.) There you go love.

Huw Thank you.

Lisa Now the game's very simple Thomas. Huw will pick a card, and on it might be a film, a book, a song, whatever. And without speaking he has to mime it to /

Elin I think he might have played it before Mum.

Lisa Very possible Elin, but everybody plays it differently.

/ Whoever guesses correctly, then it's their turn to pick. The person who has the most cards at the end wins. Make sense?

Thomas Yes.

Lisa Great. Right, Huw, you ready?

Huw Umm.

Lisa Come on then.

Huw *picks a card out of the box, looks at it and is about to start when –*

Lisa Stand up.

Huw *stands. Takes a deep breath. He mimes that it's a film.*

Elin/Lisa It's a film /

Lisa That's the sign for a film Thomas.

Thomas Right.

Huw *mimes that it's a one-word film.*

Lisa One word.

Elin Castaway!

Beat.

Huw Yeah . . .

Lisa What?

Elin Really? /

Lisa You cheated! /

Elin No I never /

Lisa / There's no way that you /

Elin What can I say, I'm just that good.

Elin *goes to grab a card.*

Lisa (*to* **Huw**) Have another go love.

Elin But /

Lisa Let him have another go!

Elin But that's not /

Lisa It was a practice round.

Elin No it /

Lisa Please!

Elin But /

Lisa Please Elin.

Elin . . . Fine . . .

Beat.

Lisa Go on then love, choose another.

Huw *picks another card out of the box, looks at it, takes a deep breath and mimes that it's a film.*

All It's a film.

Huw *mimes that it's a book.*

All And a book.

Lisa (*to* **Thomas**) That's the sign for a book / Thomas.

Elin Lord of the Rings /

Lisa Elin!

Huw *shakes his head.*

Elin Aw . . .

Lisa Not so lucky this time.

Huw *mimes that six words make up the title.*

Thomas Six words.

Lisa God it's a long one.

Huw *mimes 'first word'.*

All First word.

Huw *mimes 'One', which is the same mime as 'first word'.*

Thomas/Elin First word . . .

Lisa Yes love we know it's the first word.

Huw No it's /

Elin He spoke /

Lisa Elin.

Elin It's against the rules.

Lisa Since / when?

Huw Don't be such a motor.

Elin Motor?

Huw (*smiles at* **Thomas**) Yeah . . .

Elin What /

Lisa Just . . .

Elin What does that /

Lisa Go again love.

Huw *mimes 'first word'.*

All First word.

Huw *mimes 'One' which again looks like 'first word'.*

Lisa Yes love we know it's the first bloody /

Thomas One.

Huw *gives* **Thomas** *the thumbs up.*

Lisa Looks like you're getting the hang of it love.

Huw *mimes 'second word'.*

All Second word.

The second word is 'Flew' which **Huw** *mimes; every time they guess incorrectly* **Huw** *shakes his head.*

Elin Bird /

Thomas Flap /

Lisa Fly /

Thomas Float /

Elin Pigeon /

Lisa Pigeon?

Elin He looks like a pigeon.

Lisa Don't be so /

Huw *mimes 'sounds like'.*

Thomas Sounds like.

Huw *points at himself. For every incorrect guess* **Huw** *shakes his head.*

Elin Head /

Lisa Hair /

Thomas Huw.

Huw *nods.*

Lisa Well done /

Thomas Blue /

Elin New /

Thomas Loo /

Elin Flew! /

One Flew Over the Cuckoo's Nest.

Huw Yes.

Elin Get in!

Elin *grabs a card out of the box.*

Elin You better keep up Mum. You're flagging a bit in your old age.

Lisa Here she goes again /

Elin What now? /

Lisa Putting me down /

Elin I wasn't putting you /

Lisa Making me feel useless /

Elin It was a /

Lisa Just because she guessed correctly /

Elin Well I did didn't / I

Lisa With her fancy pants degree /

Huw Mum /

Lisa / And her great London job.

Huw Don't /

Lisa 'Quorn is actually worse for you than chicken' /

Elin I /

Lisa 'It's all processed' /

Huw Let's not /

Lisa 'It's not natural' /

Huw Please /

Lisa 'In London we' /

Elin I was joking /

Lisa Well maybe you should do us all a favour and piss off back there.

Huw Mum!

Lisa / You've overstayed your welcome.

Elin I /

Lisa Because we didn't need you then /

Elin I was /

Lisa And we don't need you now /

Elin Mum /

Lisa I mean if you hadn't decided to come home for the weekend /

Elin Fuck you!

Elin *gets up and exits through to the kitchen.*

Lisa Elin.

Where are you / going.

Elin come back!

Elin!

Sorry I /

I'll just . . .

I won't be a moment.

Lisa *follows* **Elin**.

Silence.

Huw Sorry about that . . .

Thomas It's fine.

Huw They're always at each other's /

Thomas *grabs* **Elin***'s cigarettes.*

Thomas Mind if I?

Huw Oh. No.

Thomas Thanks.

Thomas *goes to the back door.*

Thomas It's locked.

Huw Oh it's just . . .

Huw *hands* **Thomas** *the key from the shelf, he unlocks it.*

Thomas Thanks.

Thomas *puts the cigarette in his mouth and lights up.*

Thomas Want one?

Huw Oh, no, my /

Thomas Asthma?

Huw Yeah.

Thomas *smokes.*

Thomas I must be getting off soon.

Huw Off?

Thomas Home.

Huw Oh.

Yeah.

Silence.

Huw *watches* **Thomas** *smoking.*

Huw I . . . I always remember seeing you smoking behind the cul-de-sacs.

Thomas What?

Huw You know at /

Thomas Did everybody know?

Huw Uh /

Thomas Fuck, thought I'd kept it a secret.

Huw Well . . . well clearly you didn't keep it very well.

Thomas Clearly. You'll be telling me what car I drove next.

Silence.

Huw Can I . . . can I ask you a question?

Thomas Sure.

Huw How come . . . how come I knew about my nickname but, but Elin didn't know about hers?

Thomas Well I . . . I suppose . . . yours is . . .

Huw Nice?

Thomas Yeah. No need to keep it private, see.

Thomas *snubs out his cigarette, pops some chewing gum in his mouth and re-enters the house.*

Huw It means bird by the way.

Thomas What does?

Huw Aderyn.

Thomas I see.

Huw Yeah.

Thomas . . . I thought it was a secret?

Huw It was but, but there's no point in secrets unless you share them.

Thomas Suppose.

Thomas *begins to change back into his own shirt.*

Thomas Why did you go with that?

Huw What?

Thomas Bird?

Huw Well because . . .

I dunno.

Beat.

Huw I was sad to hear about your dad.

Thomas My dad?

Huw Yeah.

Thomas How did you /

Huw / I heard you telling Elin.

Thomas Right.

Beat.

Huw How did he . . . ?

Thomas Cancer.

Beat.

Huw Do you miss him?

Thomas . . . Yeah, of course.

It gets easier though. Or, or you just get used to it.

Huw Well that's . . . that's good to know.

Beat.

Thomas What about you? What about your dad?

Huw . . . What about him?

Thomas Where is he?

Huw . . . Away.

Thomas Really?

Huw . . . Yeah.

Thomas But, where?

Huw Just . . . away.

Thomas But /

Huw He got sick.

Thomas Right.

Huw And I . . .

Thomas Used to look after him?

Huw . . . I guess. And now . . .

Thomas Now?

Huw He's gone.

Beat.

Thomas How was that?

Looking after him?

Huw Fine I guess.

Thomas Fine?

Huw Yeah, I mean . . . it was easy.

Thomas Easy?

Huw Yeah I . . . I just had to make sure he washed and ate and things /

Thomas Right /

Huw Most of the time we were able to do stuff together around the house.

Thomas / Most of the time?

Huw . . . Well he . . . he . . . he has these aggressive turns.

Thomas Turns?

Huw He never used to but . . . 'it' makes him angry /

Thomas What does?

Huw No /

Thomas What's wrong with him?

Huw It makes him scared, like a . . . like a wounded animal fighting to survive.

I always think . . . if you, if you think of a baby. How they kick, how they scream when they're scared. That's what Dad is like. But he isn't a baby he's a man, a strong man.

One minute he'd be laughing, joking around and the next he'd be . . . Mum used to lock him in. Lock the doors, even if we were in 'cause, 'cause she was worried he'd try to get away.

And he'd scream, scream for us to let him out.

He'd grab me, by the wrists, and, and I would try to pull away but . . . but I couldn't . . . So I'd hide myself in the bathroom and pray, pray for him to calm down. And eventually he always did.

I used to take him out. Take him down to Llansteffan, down to the coast. He loved it there, for a couple of hours it was like having him back.

But this one time he . . .

We were, we were on our way up to the castle. Elin was home for the weekend so she came with us and he . . . he had one of his turns, but, but this time there was nowhere for me to hide and he . . .

He . . .

(*Clearly upset.*) I'm sorry, I /

Thomas No. No don't be sorry.

Huw I don't talk about it.

Thomas It's fine. (*Putting a hand on* **Huw**'s *shoulder.*) It's good to talk.

Huw It's nice to have someone that listens.

Beat.

Thomas And these . . . the coastal things . . . they're /

Huw Reminders I guess. They're . . . they're more for Mum now.

Thomas In what way?

Huw Well they . . . I dunno I guess . . . I guess they help. Make her feel like he's still at home.

Beat.

Thomas I think . . . I think you need to try to move on.

Huw What?

Thomas All of you.

Huw Why?

Thomas Because . . . because grief it . . . it ruins a place and . . . and having reminders like this it . . .

Huw What?

Thomas . . . It doesn't help.

Beat.

Huw But . . . but Mum she . . . she needs them.

Thomas No she doesn't.

Huw She does.

Thomas She'll understand.

Huw She won't.

Thomas She /

Huw She's not as . . . she's not as strong as she looks.

Thomas But you are.

Huw . . . What?

Thomas You're strong.

Huw . . . I'm not.

Thomas You are.

Huw I'm just /

Thomas The way you helped your father. The way you looked after him. That takes a lot more strength than you think. And I should know. You need to give yourself more credit.

Huw But I /

Thomas Believe in yourself a bit more.

Huw Mum she's /

Thomas I was like you once. Quiet. Shy. Gentle. But . . . but I always knew what I wanted to do so I went out there and got it. Built myself up. Made something of my life and . . . and that's what I want you to do little Blue. Put yourself first, try to move on, live your /

Huw *goes in for a kiss. Their lips meet but then* **Thomas** *pushes him away.*

Thomas No.

Huw But /

Thomas I'm sorry /

Huw But you . . .

Thomas I didn't mean to /

Huw But /

Thomas For you to think that /

Huw I /

Thomas To lead you /

Huw But /

Thomas . . . I just . . .

Huw Mum she /

Thomas I'm not /

Huw I don't understand /

Elin *enters followed by* **Lisa**.

Elin She is fucking insane.

Lisa Elin /

Huw I /

Elin (*finding it hysterical*) Listen to this right! She thought . . .

Lisa There's no need to /

Elin I can't fucking believe this . . . she thought /

Lisa Don't /

Huw But /

Elin / That I invited you over to try and set you up with him.

Thomas What /

Elin How fucking mad is that?

Lisa Don't blame this on me.

Thomas I /

Lisa You encouraged it.

Elin What? When?

Lisa Earlier when you . . . /

Elin You're fucking crackers.

Lisa I'm not.

Elin You are!

Huw Why are you /

Lisa I'd asked you to keep a look out /

Elin Yeah /

Lisa And I thought he was, you know /

Elin Gay?

Lisa Yes /

Thomas What /

Elin Why? /

Lisa 'Cause he'd given him a fucking nickname.

Elin What /

Thomas But . . . /

Elin A nickname?

Thomas Well I . . . /

Elin What nickname?

Lisa And if that isn't suggestive then I don't know what / is.

Elin Suggestive?

Lisa Yes . . .

Elin What do you mean suggestive?

Lisa Well you know . . .

Elin No /

Lisa Well if he didn't come here for Huw /

Huw I don't /

Lisa Then why the bloody hell is he here?

Beat.

Elin Well, because . . .

Lisa Because?

Elin Because I wanted to . . .

Lisa Because you wanted to what?

Elin You know . . .

Lisa No.

Elin Well . . . doesn't matter.

Lisa Yes it does.

Elin No it doesn't /

Lisa Why's he here?

Elin Because I wanted to fuck him.

Beat.

Lisa Fuck him?

Elin Yes.

Huw What /

Lisa Why? /

Thomas Well /

Elin / I thought you'd be out visiting Dad /

Huw I don't /

Elin I didn't know you'd come back early /

Lisa Right /

Elin That you'd actually meet him /

Thomas Oh /

Elin / So I thought it'd be safe.

Huw I thought that he was /

Lisa Safe?

Elin Yeah.

Lisa So it's my fault is it?

Elin What? No.

Lisa Going to blame me /

Elin That's not what I /

Lisa But that's what you do isn't it? Always putting the blame onto someone else.

Elin I didn't / mean

Lisa Because it's never your fault is it?

Elin Mum /

Lisa Nothing's ever Elin's fault, because she's too high and mighty with her first class degree to ever get anything wrong.

Elin (*she goes to leave*) Fuck off.

Lisa Fuck off?

Elin Yes.

Lisa Why?

Elin Because it's boring.

Lisa Because it's true.

Thomas (*to* **Huw**) Look, don't you worry about /

Lisa I mean look at your brother. Look what you've done to him.

Elin (*coming back into the room*) You're just jealous.

Lisa Jealous?

Elin Because I went to university /

Lisa What? /

Elin Because I got out of this place /

Lisa I'm /

Elin Because /

Lisa Because you left us to deal with it all /

Elin What /

Lisa Look after your father /

Elin Wait /

Lisa Fucking struggle /

Elin That's not /

Lisa Yes Elin, I'm really jealous of that.

Thomas I think /

Elin You told me you were coping /

Lisa What /

Elin / That you were dealing with it.

Thomas That maybe I should /

Elin That you were fine.

Lisa Well that didn't mean /

Elin You never asked me to come back /

Lisa I /

Elin Because you didn't want me /

Lisa I did /

Elin Don't / lie

Lisa I prayed for you to come back /

Elin Fuck / off

Lisa / But at the same time, no, I didn't want you to, because you'd got out, got away, you were living your dream and that filled me with so much joy.

Elin Bullshit /

Lisa But a little bit of thought for us once in a while /

Huw Mum let's /

Lisa Was that too much to ask for?

Elin You saying I didn't think about you? /

Lisa Well /

Elin That I didn't want to come back?

Lisa I don't know what /

Elin Of course I did /

Lisa Did you? /

Elin Yes.

Lisa Then why / didn't you?

Elin Because I couldn't /

Lisa Here we go / (another excuse)

Elin Because this place, this place is ruined.

Lisa Oh please /

Elin It is.

Lisa I /

Elin Because every time I'm here I think of him.

Lisa That's not / true.

Elin Because his disease, his disease has not only taken him away but ruined everything else.

Lisa I don't want to talk about / it

Elin Even the coast is ruined now because it makes me think of him.

Lisa Elin /

Elin Every memory I have of him is ruined, 'cause all I can see is the man he is instead of the man he was.

Lisa I don't want to / talk about it.

Elin Sitting there in that place /

Lisa Please /

Elin Wearing other people's clothes /

Lisa I /

Elin No idea of where he is, of who you are /

Lisa I don't /

Elin He doesn't even know his own name!

Lisa Elin /

Elin But you've never asked have you? You've never once thought about me or Huw. How much we're hurting. How much we miss him. Because you're too caught up in your own tragedy to notice anyone else's.

Silence.

Thomas I . . . I must be getting off.

Elin No /

Thomas No. No, no I've . . .

I've got a busy day tomorrow and /

Elin But /

Thomas I call ya.

Beat.

Thomas (*to* **Lisa**) Thank you for a . . . lovely evening.

Lisa My /

Thomas Anyway I'll . . .

Thomas *goes to open the back door, but it's locked.*

Lisa Let me.

Thomas No it's . . .

Thomas *tries to unlock it, but it's a struggle.*

Lisa Be careful it's /

Unlocking the door.

Thomas There.

Anyway I'll . . . thanks again.

Thomas *exits.*

Silence.

Lisa *goes to the door, it won't lock.*

Lisa It's . . .

Lisa *struggles.*

Lisa Fuck.

Elin *goes to exit, taking a bottle of wine with her.*

Lisa Huw will you /

Where you going?

Elin . . . to explain to /

Lisa Going to run away from this too?

Elin I'm /

Huw Mum /

Lisa Run away from your guilt?

Elin Let's not /

Lisa What would your father say?

Elin Well he's not here is he?

Lisa And whose fault is that?

Beat.

Elin That's not fair Mum. That is not fair.

Lisa Not fair?

Elin No /

Lisa I tell you what's not fair.

Elin It wasn't my /

Lisa Do you want to know what happened today when I went to see him?

Elin You can't /

Lisa Do you?

Elin I /

Lisa They pulled me aside when I got to the ward. Before I'd even had a chance to say hello. Dragged me into a little office. And they told me, they told me, that he won't be getting any funding. Not a penny.

And do you know what that means Elin? It means the State is going to take everything to pay for his care. They'll start with the house. They'll take his half, which means I'll never be able to afford to sell. Which means I'll be trapped here forever.

Huw Mum /

Lisa Then they'll go for his savings. His savings that were meant for you. For Huw. That he worked so hard for. They'll take and take and take until there is nothing left. So don't you dare talk to me about 'fair' because this, this is all your fault!

Elin No it's not.

Lisa Yes it is.

Elin We couldn't cope.

Lisa Yes we could!

Huw No we couldn't!

Lisa Don't you start /

Huw It's not Elin's fault.

Lisa Don't you dare side with her.

Huw You don't know what happened that day.

Lisa Of course I do.

Huw No you don't.

Lisa He forgot where he was. He forgot who you two were /

Huw No /

Elin Huw /

Lisa And he smacked her in the face! He was doing it all the time. If she'd been home more she'd have expected it.

Huw That's /

Lisa But she hadn't been, so she panicked /

Huw / That's /

Lisa Rang the hospital and then they took him away.

Huw That's not what happened.

Lisa Isn't it?

Huw No /

Elin Huw /

Lisa No?

Elin Don't /

Lisa Then what did happen?

Elin Huw /

Huw / We decided to go up to the castle /

Lisa Spare me the details /

Huw Along the path, through the fields /

Elin This isn't the time to /

Huw There's a little area off route Dad showed Elin once . . .

Lisa I know all this /

Huw She sneaked off to have a smoke whilst we carried on up the hill.

Elin Mum doesn't need to /

Huw Then she came back to find us.

Elin Huw /

Huw We were way ahead of her by now.

Elin We agreed /

Huw But then Dad had one of his turns.

Elin No /

Huw Trying to get away.

Elin Don't /

Huw I was shouting after him 'Dad! Dad dere nôl!'

Elin Stop /

Huw But he wasn't coming back.

Elin Please /

Huw When I caught up with him I tried to get him to slow down . . .

Elin Don't /

Huw And then he turned on me, fast as lightning, grabbed me by the shoulders and /

Elin Huw /

Huw Kissed me. On the mouth. And it wasn't a kiss like a father should give his son.

Elin was running by this point, running up the hill and I was screaming, screaming at him to stop but he didn't know, he couldn't know, he didn't understand.

You see she had no other choice Mum. She had to ring someone because we just couldn't cope.

Silence.

Lisa Why didn't you tell me?

Elin I was . . . I thought /

Huw Because she was trying to help.

Silence.

Elin (*going to comfort* **Lisa**) Mum let's . . .

Lisa (*she smiles*) He thought you were me.

Elin What /

Lisa That's what happened.

Elin . . . No.

Lisa That's what he was thinking.

Elin Mum.

Lisa He mistook Huw for me.

Elin We don't need to /

Lisa Because his sickness has taken everything but it couldn't take his love. Nothing could ever take that. Because he loves me /

Elin Mum /

Lisa And he knows that he loves me.

Elin Mum.

Lisa No Elin, no.

Elin I want to help you.

Lisa I don't need your help.

Elin Yes. Yes you do.

Lisa No.

Elin There's no need to pretend that / everything is OK.

Elin *tries to comfort* **Lisa.**

Lisa Get off me!

Lisa *slaps* **Elin.**

Huw Mum /

Elin I /

Beat.

Lisa I'm . . . I'm sorry Elin /

I didn't mean /

I just . . .

I miss him.

Beat.

Elin I know.

Lisa I miss him so much.

Elin So do we Mum. So do we.

Lisa It's not fair Elin.

Elin I know Mum. I know.

Huw *goes to the collection, taking a shell.*

Lisa I . . . I just wanted to do the right thing /

Elin We know you did.

Lisa For you both to be cared for.

Elin And we are Mum . . . by you.

But, but you have to be strong now, yeah? Cause we don't want you to be like this.

Lisa I /

Huw *smashes the shell.*

Elin What are you doing?

Huw I /

Elin What the fuck are you doing?

Huw It's not healthy.

Elin What /

Huw Tearing ourselves apart. Living like this /

Elin Huw /

Lisa But you /

Huw / We've got to try to move on.

Beat.

Lisa Move on?

Huw He's gone Mum.

Huw *takes another shell from the collection.*

Lisa What?

Huw He's . . . He's gone.

Lisa Don't say that.

Huw But /

Lisa Don't you dare say that.

Huw But it's true Mum.

Lisa No it's not.

Huw It is /

Lisa But he's still alive.

Huw But he's not what he was.

Lisa But he knows who I am.

Beat.

Huw . . . No he doesn't.

Lisa Yes he does.

Huw His disease /

Lisa It's not a disease.

Huw Yes it is.

Lisa (*taking the hourglass from the shelf*) I won't let you do this!

Huw But you have to!

Beat.

You . . . you have to be strong now Mum.

Lisa No.

Huw You can do it.

Lisa I can't!

Huw Yes . . . yes you can /

Lisa No.

Huw I know you can.

Lisa I can't.

Huw Because you are, you know . . . you are as strong as you look.

Beat.

Lisa I'm not /

Huw Stop putting yourself down /

Lisa I'm /

Huw Isn't that what you're always telling me?

Lisa . . . Yes . . . but /

Huw Now it's your turn to do the same.

Beat.

Lisa We're not doing this.

Huw Mum /

Lisa Tell him Elin /

Elin I . . .

Huw Go on Mum /

Lisa No /

Huw But /

Lisa I'm not ready.

Huw Yes . . .

Yes you are.

Lisa I'm not.

Huw Do it for me. Do it for us /

Lisa Elin /

Huw Do it for Dad.

Beat.

Lisa I . . . /

I'm scared.

Huw I know Mum, so am I . . . but . . . but we will be here for you.

Won't we Elin?

Elin . . . Yes . . . (*She takes the shell off* **Huw**.) We will.

Huw And we'll . . . we'll look after you . . . if you let us. Because that's what Dad would want. But . . . but these reminders. We don't need them.

Lisa Yes . . . yes we do.

Huw We don't. Because . . . because Dad will always be with us.

And you, you will always be his 'Cariad'. But . . .

But at the same time . . .

He would want you . . .

He would want me . . .

A breeze travels through the house, blowing open the door.

He would want us . . .

To be /

Lisa *pulls the stopper out of the hourglass.*

Huw *looks at her. He smiles.*

Lisa *goes to empty the hourglass . . .*

Blackout.

End.

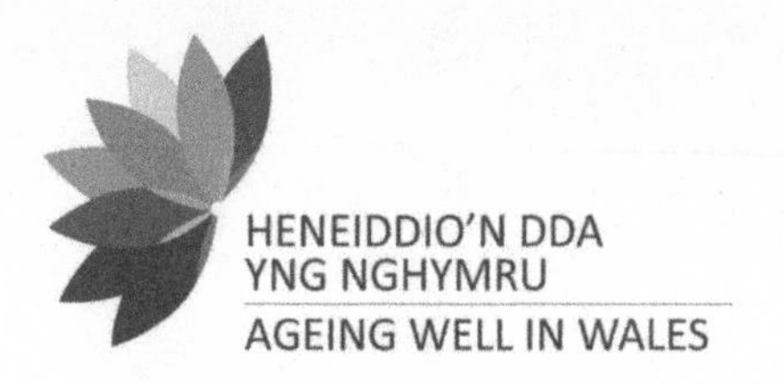

Heneiddio'n Dda yng Nghymru

Mae Heneiddio'n Dda yng Nghymru yn rhaglen bartneriaeth sy'n cael ei chynnal a'i chadeirio gan Gomisiynydd Pobl Hŷn Cymru.

Rydyn ni i gyd eisiau sicrhau mai Cymru yw'r lle gorau yn y byd i heneiddio ynddo. Mae Heneiddio'n Dda yng Nghymru yn dod ag unigolion a chymunedau, a'r sectorau cyhoeddus, preifat a gwirfoddol at ei gilydd. Rydyn ni'n gweithio gyda'n gilydd i wneud Cymru yn wlad o gymunedau sy'n ystyriol o oedran, lle caiff lleisiau pobl hŷn eu clywed ac y caiff pobl eu cefnogi i barhau i wneud y pethau sy'n bwysig iddyn nhw wrth fynd yn hŷn.

I gael rhagor o wybodaeth, ewch i **www.ageingwellinwales.com**, anfonwch e-bost atom yn **ageingwell@olderpeoplewales.com** neu ffoniwch ni ar **029 20 445 030**.

Ageing Well in Wales

Ageing Well in Wales is a national partnership programme hosted and chaired by the Older People's Commissioner for Wales.

We want to make Wales the best place in the world to grow older. Ageing Well in Wales brings together individuals and communities with public, private and voluntary sectors. We work together to make Wales a nation of age-friendly communities, where the voices of older people are heard, and where people are supported to continue to do the things that matter to them as they get older.

For more information, visit **www.ageingwellinwales.com**, email **ageingwell@olderpeoplewales.com** or phone us on **029 20 445 030**.